Rabbit

Amazing Fun Facts and Pictures about Rabbit for Kids

Gaia Carlo

I am a rabbit.

I have big pointed ears.

I like to live with other rabbits.

I eat and hop all day.

I love people and I love kids.

I can be a good pet.

I have big teeth that I use to chew carrots.

I have big bright eyes and I can see well at night.

I can hear well, too.

I get lonely when I am alone.

I like to dig holes in the ground.

I am small but I am heavy.

I can live up to 16 years.

My teeth grow bigger and bigger.

I get grumpy when you get into my space.

I like to sleep, eat, and play.

I purr when I am happy.

I also run and hop around when I am happy.

I have sharp nails.

I am afraid of bigger animals like tigers, lions, panthers, and hyenas.

I lick my friends to let them know that I love them.

I can sleep with my eyes open.

Made in the USA
Middletown, DE
13 April 2019